kerry lewis

Eating for Your Aura

Rodney K Press

copyright @2024 Kerry Lewis

publisher Rodney K Press
www.rodneykpress.com
food photography and page 151 Dusty Hoskovec
Hoskovecphotography.com
(dragon/angel/gnome)
photos of Kerry pages 148,149 @kitara_krueger
(wizard/dragon/mermaid)
graphic design and hardcover layout Kerry Lewis
(fairy/wizard/dragon)

All rights reserved. No part of this publication may be reproduced, distributed, or transmitted in any form or by any means, including photocopying, recording, or other electronic or mechanical methods, without the prior written permission of the publisher, except in case of brief quotations embodied in critical reviews and certain other noncommercial uses permitted by copyright law.
ISBN 978-1-960111-18-0

gratitude

i would like to express gratitude to my
family, friends and clients

who have found the playfulness, humor and healing in resonating as a
dragon elf gnome fairy angel wizard merperson star

you have sparked me to create this colorful book and have brought me

and

Eating for Your Aura

My name is Kerry and I see auras.

As an intuitive energy healer, I use the gift of seeing auras to empower people.

Why eat for your aura?

Your aura can offer insight into which living foods of the rainbow best nourish your body, mind, and spirit.

Take the aura energy quiz!

I have designed an enlightening and fun aura quiz that enables you to access the colorful energies in your aura, empowering you to make intuitive choices which serve your unique self best.

Get to know your spirited, colorful, playful, intuitive self

The quiz will then match you to recipes for your unique aura.

Are you ready?

let's UNLOCK your aura energies!

Taking your time, settle in with pen and paper. You will be using your intuition to sense your energies within eight aura quizzes.

Each quiz has 7 statements. Tally one mark for each time you answer YES to a statement. After completing all eight of the quizzes, compile your top three ranking aura categories (those scoring closest to 7) to determine which 3 auras you resonate with the most.

your aura will be a unique blend of

- ★ dragon aura ★
- ★ fairy aura ★ angel aura ★
- ★ elf aura ★ merperson aura ★
- ★ wizard aura ★ star aura ★
- ★ gnome aura ★

match your aura to the color recipes

After completing the quizzes, turn to the KEY to unlock your aura energies with your top matching aura chapters. There you will find welcome letters, living food recipes, and tips! I have created these special recipes for best nourishing your colorful self.

nourishing aura recipes

And have fun sharing the aura quiz with family and friends! Knowing which recipes are nourishing for your loved ones can be enlightening and empowering.

contents

aura energy quiz 1
aura key 11

gnome aura & recipes 13
merperson aura & recipes 27
wizard aura & recipes 41
elf aura & recipes 57
angel aura & recipes 69
yellow star aura & recipes 83
fairy aura & recipes 97
dragon aura & recipes 111

color energies 125
living foods in color 139
edible flowers 147

connect with kerry 151

aura
energy quiz

aura A

- My dream house is a cabin in the woods where I can build fires and cook/make/fix things with my hands.

- I find joy in feeding forest animals such as birds, rabbits, and deer.

- Heights scare me.

- I prefer a good road trip as opposed to flying so I can experience the beauty of the land while remaining on the ground.

- I embrace living where there are 4 distinct seasons.

- I have an affinity for rich, dark, shady soil where mushrooms and moss can grow.

- I feel the need to have a dog or be around dogs as much as possible.

_/7

aura B

- My favorite style of eating includes talking, laughing, and lengthy communing around a round table.

- Organizing big events and gatherings nourishes my soul.

- My spirit desires to live near a warm sea ALL year round.

- My ultimate dining setting is eating outdoors at a casual fish shack with the sounds of seagulls and rolling ocean waves nearby.

- My favorite foods are from the sea.

- I can feel my heart filled with joy when I am submerged or floating in water.

- I feel a deep connection with sea creatures as though I am part of their family.

_/7

aura C

- I have a connection with receiving psychic messages.

- I have dark circles under my eyes and I am deeply exhausted.

- I may be prone to having acidity in my stomach.

- The color purple gives me a sense of calm or I have an aversion to purple.

- I believed I was magic when I was little.

- I can easily see through other's problems and sense possible outcomes.

- I feel as though my soul has lived on this earth for eons and not much surprises me.

_/7

aura D

- I was born with a twinkle in my eye.

- I'm naughty by nature and continually look for playful ways to bend/break the rules.

- If I had to take away the jokester part of my personality it would deplete my zest for living.

- I feel as though I must continually be on the move or I may get caught.

- The color bright lime green exhilarates me more than all of the other colors.

- Knowing that there is a tree or a corner to zip around or hide behind feels comforting.

- I am the KING of tricking others without their knowing.

_/7

aura E

- I am overly giving to others and often neglect self-care.

- I need pastries, cakes, or bread when I'm stressed so that I don't DIE!

- I crave foods high in iron (including red meat) to stabilize me so I don't feel lost and dizzy.

- Feeling the negative energy of people in a room that I walk into comes way too easy.

- I seem to have more empathy for people than others do.

- I have a special connection to harps, bells, white clouds, or white feathers.

- Babies remind me of little angels and hold a special place in my heart.

_/7

aura F

- My favorite color is yellow.

- I must have bananas as a source of life-force energy.

- I prefer the shade, as opposed to being exposed to the direct rays of the high, bright, noon-time sun.

- Electronic or synthesizer music makes me feel amazing!

- I have an interest in astrology.

- Technology, solar energy, and being an entrepreneur are all strong passions of mine.

- I have longer fingers than most others.

_/7

aura G

- My favorite way of eating is snacking on small meals throughout the entire day.

- I need to be outdoors in natural sunlight as much as possible every day.

- I have strong physical or allergic reactions to fluorescent lighting, air conditioning, synthetic chemicals, and pesticides.

- I must have indoor plants in my home or it feels empty of life.

- I am attracted to concocting homemade remedies of lotions and potions, stews, and brews.

- Honey and/or chocolate feel medicinal to me.

- I prefer being around plants and animals over humans.

_/7

aura H

- My dream is to fly.

- My best sleep is in a cave-like dark room.

- I am mesmerized by the deep red flames of a fire more than the blue flames.

- Ancient castles and dwellings hold a special place in my heart.

- I LOVE hoarding rocks and shiny golden objects in a special treasure chest.

- Enjoying warm food served on handmade pottery or in wooden bowls is the best way to nourish myself.

- I have an important mission of spreading love and goodness while living on this earth.

_/7

key

Here is where you will find the energies correlating with auras A, B, C, D, E, F, G, and H from the quiz. If you scored high in the aura H category, you will find yourself vibing with dragon energies. You have a lot of love to give and your recipes are in the dragon chapter. If you scored high in aura G, you have fairy energy. You need to nibble on fruits and flowers all day long and your recipes are in the fairy chapter. If you scored high in aura F, you have yellow star energy. You shine bright as the sun and you will find how to replenish your energies in the star chapter. If you scored high in aura E, you have angel energy and need to ground yourself with red and white foods. Your recipes are in the angel section. If you scored high in aura D, then you have elf energy! You need to fill up with bright green living foods to match your bright green aura. So look for your recipes in the lime-colored elf chapter. If you scored high in aura C, you have purple wizard energy! You need to eat purple and blue foods to replenish your purple aura, so look for your recipes in the wizard chapter. If you scored high in aura B, then you have mer-person energies. You are a hard worker and you will find your sea and mediterranean sun-loving recipes in the mer-person chapter. And if you scored high in aura A, then you have gnome energy! Gnomes need to prepare recipes with beautiful, root-colored foods from the earth and you can find everything you need to know in the gnome chapter.

Welcome to your gnome aura!

First of all, gnomes are lovely!

Your energy is the most grounded because you possess a deep affinity for the soil. Your energy stems from the dark, rich nutrients found in the earth, and gazing into a crackling fire fills your heart. Your living space is warm and cozy, and your kitchen is full of good ingredients. Sweeping the floor and feeding your dog special food feels good to you, and you enjoy treating birds to berries, nuts, and seeds.

You are warm-hearted and energize yourself by staying close to home. You love working with your hands, and they pour out love when you create art, fix things, and prepare homemade meals for family and friends.

To nourish your gnome-like self the best, the living foods you need the most are from the ground up. Root vegetables of all colors are best, replenishing your body's energies and earthy spirit. Oven-bake your orange sweet potatoes, red beets, golden potatoes, white turnips, and purple carrots, green Brussels sprouts, and orange pumpkin, and gather green spinach and red bell peppers. Bake veggies in a homemade chicken pot pie and feel your heart sing.

Picking strawberries and apples is in your nature, as well as baking scrumptious oatmeal cakes. For breakfast, enjoy eggs, bacon, and oatmeal pancakes served with homemade butter and real maple syrup. Embrace your gnome energies and have fun creating these recipes for your family and friends.

sweet potato bird nest bowls

4 whole sweet potatoes, pierced on top with a knife
4 beets, peeled and cubed, drizzled with avocado oil
2 bunches broccolini, cut lengthwise into 2 " pieces
½ pound maple bacon cut into bite-sized pieces
Garnishes of shredded smoked gouda cheese, edible flowers, chives, and toasted sunflower seeds

Preheat the oven to 375 degrees. Line two pans with parchment paper. At the same time, roast the pierced whole sweet potatoes in the oven on one pan and the cubed beets drizzled with avocado oil and salt on the other pan.
When the beets are tender after about 20 or more minutes, remove from the oven and set aside. When the sweet potatoes are very tender and smell caramel-ly after another 30-60 minutes, scoop the sweet potatoes out of the skins, mash with a fork or hand blender until creamy, and set aside.

To prepare the broccolini, chop off the bottom portions of the stems and slice any very large florets in half lengthwise. Drizzle some avocado oil in a sautè pan and stir fry the broccolini until crisp-tender, about 3-4 minutes. Then add a bit of water and salt to steam for 2 more minutes until the broccolini is bright green and tender. Remove from the heat and set aside. To prepare the bacon, sautè in a pan until crispy. Remove from the pan, dry the bacon pieces on a paper towel, and set aside.

To make the bird nests, scoop the mashed sweet potatoes evenly into 4 serving bowls. Add layers of bacon, broccolini, and beets, and then garnish with shredded smoked gouda cheese, chives, edible flowers, and toasted sunflower seeds. Serve with warm crusty bread and butter.

oatmeal love cake

1 ¼ cup water
1 stick butter
1 cup oatmeal

1 cup white sugar
1 cup brown sugar
1 teaspoon baking soda
½ teaspoon salt
½ teaspoon cinnamon
1 ½ cups flour
1 teaspoon vanilla
2 eggs

coconut topping:
½ cup powdered sugar
6 tablespoons soft butter
2 teaspoons vanilla
½ cup shredded coconut
¼ cup cream

Turn on the oven to 350 degrees and prepare a buttered and floured bundt cake pan or 9 x 13 pan. Set aside. Then add the first 3 ingredients to a small pot (water, butter, and oatmeal.) Cook over medium heat and bring to a boil. Remove the oatmeal mixture from the stovetop and let sit for about 20 minutes.

In a large bowl, mix the white sugar, brown sugar, baking soda, salt, cinnamon, flour, vanilla, and eggs. Then add the oatmeal mixture to the flour mixture, and pour into your cake pan. If using a bundt cake pan, cook for about 50 minutes or until a toothpick comes out clean. Cool the cake for up to an hour, loosen the edges, and then carefully turn it over onto a platter. If using a 9 x 13 pan, the cake will take about 35 minutes and will stay in the pan.

To make the coconut topping:
Mix the powdered sugar, butter, vanilla, coconut, and cream in a small saucepan. Heat on the stove over medium heat for 1-2 minutes. Lovingly drizzle over the cake while the mixture is still warm so that it sinks into and around the cake.

spinach cream cheese lasagna

9 no-cook lasagna noodles
1 pound spicy Italian sausage
1 jar (24 ounces) cheesy or garlic spaghetti sauce
1 carton ricotta cheese (15 oz.)
2 cups mozzarella cheese
4 ounces cream cheese
1 package (10 ounces) frozen chopped spinach, thawed and squeezed dry
1/2 cup parmesan cheese

Preheat the oven to 350 degrees. Cook the spicy sausage in a large skillet over medium heat until cooked through. Stir in the spaghetti sauce and set aside. In a large bowl, mix the ricotta cheese, mozzarella cheese, cream cheese, and spinach.

Spread about 1 cup of the sauce mixture in a greased 9 x 13 pan. Layer with three noodles, 1 cup sauce mixture, and half of the spinach cheese mixture. Repeat layers. Then layer with the 3 remaining noodles and the remaining sauce mixture. Sprinkle with the parmesan cheese.

Cover with foil and cook for about an hour until bubbly and the noodles are tender. Remove from the oven and let sit for about 10 minutes before cutting into servings.

dining

gnomes prefer

a warm fire and warm beverages

baking moist cakes and crusty breads

a messy, full table

slow roasting meats and buttery vegetables

hosting family and friends

feeding table food to their dogs

storytelling

gnome market

beets
cinnamon
vanilla
sunflower seeds
red onion
shallot
sweet potato
spinach
parsnip
broccoli
collard greens
lasagna noodles
maple bacon
butter
potato
oatmeal
radish
brussel sprouts
maple syrup
turnips
sage
cream

merperson aura

Welcome to your merperson aura!

If you yearn to swim underwater endlessly, never needing to surface for air, your spirit finds its home in the sea. Your merperson aura reflects the energies of a hard worker, and you are happiest being active. Feeling as though you are swimming and in perpetual motion gives you a sense of being at home within yourself.

You're highly motivated, and there is nothing you can't do if you set your mind to it. You love to organize gatherings, dine in groups, and play lots of games. Finding comfort in camaraderie, collaborating with others toward common goals, is akin to swimming amidst a school of fish, gathering friends along the way.

Foods native to the Mediterranean region hold the power to re-energize your Mediterranean blue aquatic energy, embodying the essence of being kissed and ripened by the low, warm, afternoon sun. Reinvigorate and rejuvenate yourself with figs, dates, apricots, grapes, olives, lemons, cucumbers, mangoes, ancient grains, and legumes. The recipes enclosed in this chapter are designed specifically for you to feel your merperson-al best!

roasted red pepper hummus

1 can of chickpeas plus the water in the can

⅓ cup tahini paste

2 cloves garlic

2 tablespoons fresh lemon juice

½ cup roasted red peppers

2 tablespoons extra virgin olive oil

½ teaspoon salt

garnishes of finely chopped orange and red bell peppers

pita bread

Simply combine all of the ingredients in a food processor. Pulse until the consistency is creamy. Scoop into a bowl and add garnishes of finely chopped orange and red peppers on top. Serve with warm slices of pita bread.

mediterranean platter

roasted red pepper hummus
mixed greens
cherry tomatoes
kalamata olives
feta cheese
cucumber
roasted red peppers
parsley
lemon
olive oil
pita bread

Chop all of the vegetables into bite-sized pieces. Scoop the hummus into the middle of the platter and place the mixed greens around the hummus. On top of the mixed greens add the halved cherry tomatoes, olives, cucumbers, roasted red peppers, feta cheese, and parsley.

Season the platter with salt and pepper, then drizzle with lemon juice and olive oil. Serve with fresh or toasted pita bread.

vanilla fig jam

2 pounds fresh figs, cut in quarters with stems removed
1 cup sugar
juice of one lemon
1 teaspoon vanilla extract
¼ cup water

In a medium saucepan, toss in the figs, sugar, lemon, and vanilla. Cook over medium heat, stirring frequently until the sugar dissolves and the figs are juicy. Turn the heat to low, add the water, and simmer for 20 minutes, stirring occasionally until the figs are soft and the juices start to thicken.

Turn off the heat and spoon the jam into 2 small jars. Close the jars with lids and allow them to cool to room temperature. Store the jam in the refrigerator for up to two months.

The fig jam may be served on a platter with cheeses and crackers, or a tablespoon may be stirred into a cup of hot water with a few raspberries for a creamy, warm, pink drink, or served as a sweet jam on buttery toast.

dining

merpeople prefer

family style sharing

linens and wooden serving utensils

dipping bowls, large serving bowls, paella pans, woks, oval platters and soup pots

foods grown near and from the sea

wine and water with meals

large, round tables

lengthy communing

merperson market

figs
olives
chickpeas
tomato
tahini paste
extra virgin olive oil
roasted peppers
fish
dates
feta cheese
parsley
pita bread
lemons
mango
sheep's milk cheese
mixed greens
okra
greek yogurt
lentils
herbal teas

wizard aura

Welcome to your wizard aura!

Here's what wizards need to know:

Your aura might present itself in one of the many shades of purple, reflecting ancient knowledge and wisdom. Naturally psychic, you possess intuitive insights and may have magical abilities to wave your wand and make good things happen.

You may also crave fantasy books, informational podcasts, travel guides, and global recipe books more than others. However, individuals with wizard auras might feel exhausted, as though they are carrying around the weight of the world. You may feel as though you have already seen and done it all.

If you tend to feel sluggish with an acidic stomach, your aura may appear as dark purple. If not, your aura color may appear more of an indigo or a lighter shade of purple.

Regardless, you should replenish, restore, and energize your wizard self with a daily dose of purple/blue foods! The blue phytochemicals found in fruits, vegetables, and flowers can revitalize your blue/purple aura, reducing energy depletion. Adopting a pH-balanced diet (limiting fatty and acidic foods) along with blue-colored foods can work wonders in combating sluggishness and acidity.

Consider making blueberries your 'most special food friend,' along with red grapes, blackberries, purple potatoes, purple carrots, blue tomatoes, purple onion, purple cauliflower, eggplant, plums, concord grapes, blue pansies, acai berries, purple cabbage, bachelor buttons, blue flower teas, and blue honey. Replenishing with blue and purple-colored foods is akin to finding your holy grail. Enjoy the recipes crafted for you in this chapter and embrace your wizard aura!

coconut flour blueberry pancakes

1 medium sized ripe banana
3 eggs
¼ cup blueberries, fresh or frozen
3 tablespoons coconut flour
½ teaspoon baking soda
¼ teaspoon salt
coconut oil or ghee

Prepare the batter by mashing the banana in a medium-sized mixing bowl and then add in the egg. Whip with a fork until fully combined.

In a separate bowl, whisk together the coconut flour, baking soda, and salt. Pour the flour mixture into the egg mixture and whisk until fully combined. Let the batter sit for about 3-5 minutes. While it's sitting, preheat the frying pan by turning the burner to medium heat and add in some coconut oil or ghee.

Once the pan is heated, stir the blueberries into the batter and use a spoon to pour out small-sized pancakes. When bubbles begin to form, flip them or let them cook another minute if they need to firm up a little after about 3 minutes. After both sides are medium golden, enjoy eating them stacked on a plate with pure maple syrup and your favorite toppings.

salmon with blueberry sauce

2-pound salmon filet
2 tablespoons coconut oil
1 teaspoon salt
1/2 teaspoon pepper

blueberry sauce
1 cup fresh or frozen wild blueberries
juice from 2 oranges
1 tablespoon coconut oil
2 tablespoons coconut amino acids
salt and pepper
dash nutmeg
dash cinnamon

To cook the salmon, preheat the oven to 450 degrees. Arrange the filet on a baking sheet lined with parchment paper or a cast iron skillet. Drizzle with melted coconut oil and salt and pepper. Roast for about 15 minutes for well done.

To make the blueberry sauce, use a pan on medium heat. Add in the blueberries, orange juice, coconut oil, coconut amino acids, salt, pepper, nutmeg, and cinnamon. Stir everything together and mash the blueberries into the juices using a fork so that the flavors combine.

Continue to cook until the blueberry mixture has cooked down and slightly thickened, about 10-15 minutes. Spoon the sauce on the plated filets or serve on the side.

blueberry banana smoothie

2 ripe frozen bananas
1 cup frozen wild or cultivated blueberries
1 vanilla bean pod or 2 teaspoons vanilla
½ cup greek yogurt
1 cup coconut water
a shake of cinnamon
a shake of nutmeg

Blend all ingredients in a blender until smooth.

dining

wizards prefer

engaging in intellectual conversations

low lighting and a warm ambiance

listening to moody music

experiencing global foods

reading books while eating

savoring the flavors

dining alone

wizard market

banana
coconut flour
blueberries
blackberries
purple cabbage
fish
blue carrot
thyme
avocado oil
vanilla bean pod
zucchini noodles
eggplant
coconut aminos
bok choy
plums
turkey
concord grapes
purple grapes
fish sauce
shredded coconut
mustard
purple cauliflower
fennel bulb
blue potato

Welcome to your elf aura!

Have you been told that you have a twinkle in your eye? Here's what you should know about having elf energy:

Your aura shines in a vibrant lime green, perfectly mirroring your enthusiasm for being the life of every party. You embrace silliness, mischief, and playfulness, finding sheer delight in being the center of attention. Your pace is quick—scurrying, working, eating, and moving swiftly all invigorate you, especially when people take notice, allowing you to share a twinkle-eyed wave or elicit laughter.

Your aura may also embody shades like spring green, basil green, grass green, pine tree green, string bean green, or minty green. These hues reflect the vibrancy of your personality, enriched with a healthy dose of trickster, jester, hoaxer, and prankster traits. Elves are entertainers, but on the contrary, may feel exposed without the security and comfort of corners or trees to hide behind. Disappearing behind a friendly tree is key so that you don't get caught.

Given your bright green aura, replenishing your energies involves consuming vibrant, living green plants! While you might prefer lime-colored candy over greens, incorporating a daily dose of spinach, green peppers, kiwi, cucumbers or romaine lettuce is essential. Flip through these pages to discover delectable green recipes, including the goodness of hard white cheese. Eating your greens will boost your energy, ensuring you have enough zest to keep entertaining.

green beans with bacon

1 pound fresh green beans
5-6 slices thick-cut bacon
2 tablespoons butter
½ onion, finely chopped
3 cloves garlic, finely minced
1 teaspoon dried dill
1 teaspoon Italian seasoning
salt and pepper to taste
⅓ cup grated parmesan cheese

Boil the green beans in a large pot of salted water for about 8-10 minutes until tender. Drain the beans and set aside.

Cook the slices of bacon in a skillet until well done, then remove them from the skillet to a paper towel-lined plate. Pour off excess bacon drippings, reserving about 1 tablespoon left in the pan. Turning the heat to low, add the butter and allow it to brown in the pan for about 3-4 minutes. Add the onion, seasonings, and garlic, and cook for another 3-4 minutes until the onion is soft.

Place the green beans in the skillet, and continually stir while the beans absorb the flavors for another couple of minutes. Remove from the heat and top with pieces of crumbled bacon and sprinkles of parmesan cheese. Serve warm.

pico de gallo

1 cup cilantro, chopped
1 jalapeño pepper, seeded and finely minced
1 medium or large white onion, chopped
1 pound grape tomatoes, diced
2 tablespoons lime juice from 1 lime
½ teaspoon salt
⅛ teaspoon pepper

In a medium bowl, mix in the cilantro, jalapeño pepper, onion, and diced tomatoes. Stir in the lime juice and season to taste with salt and pepper.

Mix well and enjoy with chips, tacos, burritos, or nachos. You can also refrigerate covered overnight for juicier and zestier flavors.

elf basil pesto

2 cups fresh basil leaves, setting aside 3 leaves for garnish
1 cup of shredded parmesan for pesto and 1 cup for topping
½ cup olive oil
1 teaspoon salt and 1 teaspoon pepper
1 pound penne noodles
2 chicken breasts, cut into bite-sized pieces
3 cloves garlic, minced
2 tablespoons butter

To make the pesto in a food processor, add the basil and pulse a couple of times. Add 1 cup of the freshly shredded cheese and pulse a couple more times. While the food processor is running, slowly pour in the olive oil. Stop to scrape down the sides and season with the salt and pepper. Taste and flavor to perfection.

Cook the noodles to al dente and then drain out the water using a lid. Sir in 1-2 tablespoons of olive oil to coat the noodles and allow them to cool down slightly before folding in the pesto. Thoroughly combine.

Cook the chicken pieces in a pan on low heat with the butter, minced garlic, and salt and pepper. After the chicken is seasoned and cooked through, remove from the heat so it can absorb the juices. Once the chicken has come to slightly above room temperature, combine the buttery chicken with the pesto noodles. Sprinkle with the remaining cup of cheese and lightly toss. Garnish with some whole basil leaves.

dining

elves prefer

eating while driving

party style mingling

appetizers with toothpicks

cheese platters and finger foods

entertaining others while dining

drinking bevies in place of dinner

playing with food

elf market

dill
lime
cilantro
green pepper
basil
bacon
green onion
white hard cheese
green grapes
bacon
asparagus
green beans
spinach
white onion
broccolini
butter
green pears
green peas
cucumber
green apples
kiwi

angel aura

Welcome to your angel aura!

Have you ever been called an angel? It's probably because others recognize your desire to care for everyone you meet.

If you have angelic energy in your aura, you most likely put others first, and you may have been drawn into the medical, teaching, and healing arts industries. You love to lift others up, help, and heal them so that they may shine.

You are also wired to do the right thing. Following the rules is comforting and stabilizing to you, and you may secretly wish you had more energy in the day to help everyone with all that needs to be done.

However, since you have angelic energy, you may easily absorb others' negative energy. Saving everyone is exhausting, and you may be prone to be easily overwhelmed and suffer from aches and pains. This is because you are trying to carry everyone's heavy loads. Taking time for self-care may not be high on your priority list.

So, to keep yourself grounded, balanced, and fortified with strength, angel people need to eat red and white-colored foods, especially those that are rich in iron. Red and white-colored vegetables, fruits, and red meats will help stabilize, give strength, and replenish the red-colored energies in your grounding root chakra. And these foods will help support your white angel wings. Since your wings give you the power to care for others so much, fortify them with as much iron and red living food energies as you can get! Embrace your angel qualities and remember to nourish yourself so you can feel your best.

beef with cauliflower

1 tablespoon ghee or avocado oil
1 pound ground beef
1 head cauliflower
2 tablespoons red curry paste
1 tablespoon five spice powder
salt and pepper to taste
1 small bunch mint (reserving a few whole leaves)
1 (14 ounce) can coconut milk

Start by cooking 2 cups of jasmine rice in a rice cooker. Halve the cauliflower and cut little bite-sized florets off the sections until you have about 2 cups of little florets, and set aside.

Sautè the ground beef in a cast iron skillet with 1 tablespoon of ghee over medium-high heat until cooked through, and then add in the cauliflower florets. Stir in the red curry paste, five spice powder, salt, and pepper, and cook it all for 10 minutes, stirring regularly until crispy.

Chop the mint leaves in half, toss into the cauliflower mixture, then pour in the coconut milk and half a cup of water. Bring to a boil, and simmer for up to 5 minutes, seasoning to taste. Serve over a bowl of rice, and garnish with a few whole mint leaves.

yukon gold medallions

2 tablespoons avocado oil or ghee
1 pound baby Yukon Gold potatoes,
    sliced into coins, about ¼" thick
½ onion, diced
1 tablespoon freshly chopped rosemary
1 tablespoon garlic, minced
salt and pepper

preferably use a cast iron skillet

Chop the onions, mince the garlic and set aside. Slice the potatoes into coins.

Add the oil or ghee into the cast iron skillet and turn on medium heat. After slightly heating the oil, add in the potatoes and onion, and then season with rosemary, salt, and pepper.

Cook, undisturbed, until the potatoes are golden and crusty underneath, about 5-8 minutes. Flip the potatoes and cook until golden on the other sides, about 5-8 more minutes. Continue to cook, stirring occasionally, until potatoes are golden and tender. Serve warm.

crimson red fruit salad

1 cup cherries, pitted and halved
1 cup raspberries
1 cup blackberries, halved
4 cups watermelon, cubed
1 cup strawberries, sliced sideways into coins

2 tablespoons agave or honey
2 tablespoons juice and 1 teaspoon zest from
   one or two limes
1 tablespoon mint or basil, finely chopped

In a small bowl, whisk together the agave or honey, lime juice, lime zest, and finely chopped mint or basil.

In a large bowl, lightly mix the watermelon cubes, cherries, raspberries, blackberries, and strawberries. Drizzle the sweet lime dressing over the top. Lightly mix and serve immediately.

dining

angels prefer

action filled environments

secretly indulging alone in pastries, cakes, and sweet creams

eating in prayerful solitude late at night

serving others before eating

listening to nearby conversations

multi-tasking
while
dining

angel market

cherries
raspberries
rainbow chard
spinach
red meat
watermelon
potatoes
red apples
cauliflower
white onions
rosemary
strawberries
dark turkey meat
pomegranate
quinoa
radishes
legumes
tomatoes
cranberries

yellow star aura

Welcome to your yellow star aura!

Here's what your yellow star aura means:

You radiate bright energy, and your aura might exhibit a warm, golden-yellow hue, akin to the brilliance of a honey-lemon-colored sun. You thrive on achieving excellence and harbor a passion for music, technology, and mental strategies. New ideas are constantly swirling in your head.

At times, you may be prone to irritation or anxiety, perhaps due to attracting unwanted attention from those seeking to extinguish your bright yellow flame. You may feel over-exposed and irritable under a bright, shining daytime sun, often experiencing dehydration. Opt for shade and increase your water intake since you shine so brightly! Lemon water is the best choice to rejuvenate your radiant yellow flame.

Additionally, stock up on yellow sunshine-colored living foods. You need yellow bananas, yellow zucchini, orange squash, yellow bell peppers, eggs, butter, pineapple, honey, mangoes, and papayas into your diet. The yellow star recipes featured in this chapter offer delicious and simple ways for you to eat the foods that will keep your yellow candle flame from sizzling and burning out.

sunshine tortilla eggs

butter
1 large tortilla
½ cup baby spinach, roughly chopped
½ cup yellow bell pepper, cut into chunks
3 eggs
1 tablespoon green onions, finely chopped
⅛ teaspoon paprika
1 tablespoon cheddar cheese, grated
salt and pepper

Preheat the oven to 350 degrees. Roughly chop the spinach and cut the yellow pepper into small chunks. Butter a small baking dish (smaller than the tortilla) and then press the tortilla into the bottom of the dish, allowing the sides to curl up to hold the eggs.

Place the spinach and yellow pepper evenly on the tortilla and then crack the eggs on top. Sprinkle on the green onions, paprika, salt, pepper, and then the grated cheese. Place in the oven for 20 minutes until the egg whites are set.

Remove from the oven and slide onto a plate, cutting the tortilla into quarters to serve. Garnish with more chopped fresh green onion.

cinnamon maple squash

2 acorn squash
2 teaspoons avocado oil
4 tablespoons butter, divided
4 tablespoons pure maple syrup
dashes of salt
1 teaspoon ground cinnamon

Preheat the oven to 400 degrees. Cut the squash in half and arrange the cut sides up on a parchment paper-lined, rimmed baking sheet. Lightly brush the insides with the avocado oil and add a tablespoon of butter to each squash. Sprinkle with salt and cinnamon, and drizzle each with a tablespoon of maple syrup.

Roast the squash in the oven for 45-60 minutes until the flesh is tender and soft when poked with a fork. To infuse extra flavor, brush the insides of the squash after 30 minutes of baking with the maple butter juices accumulated in each squash.

Serve warm on a platter with more drizzles of maple syrup and salt if desired.

golden healing milk

heated:
4 cups almond, coconut, or oat milk
2 teaspoons ground turmeric powder
½ teaspoon ginger
1 tablespoon ghee
⅛ teaspoon black pepper
1 teaspoon ground cinnamon
¼ teaspoon cardamom
¼ teaspoon nutmeg
¼ teaspoon ground cloves

unheated:
1 teaspoon vanilla extract
2 tablespoons honey

Whisk all of the ingredients to be heated together in a large pot. Heat over medium heat just until simmering. Reduce heat to low (should just be a light simmer) then cover and let simmer for 5 minutes. Remove from heat.

Stir in the vanilla and honey and allow the milk to steep off of the heat for another 5 minutes. Serve warm or cooled over ice.

dining

yellow stars prefer

dining in air conditioning

listening to high-volume electric music

using technology while eating

drinking lots of liquid

eating sporadically and only when necessary

being served food and dining quickly

cold foods

star market

honey
turmeric
yellow bell pepper
banana
lemon
ghee
egg yolk
summer squash
star fruit
asian pears
acorn squash
golden beets
ginger root
pineapple
yellow tomato
nectarine
golden apple
pumpkin
yellow zucchini
papaya

fairy aura

Welcome to your fairy aura!

Here's what you need to know:

Fairy spirits require plenty of natural sunlight daily! Imagine your heart as a flower garden, seeking the remedies of the sun, air, earth, and water, along with honey from local bees for your soul.

Clean air, water, and organic foods are important to you, while chemicals, pesticides, fluorescent lighting, and synthetic fragrances in perfumes and candles are highly irritating to your senses. A lack of daily sunlight can leave you feeling nervous, sad, lackluster, or even depressed.

To recharge your fairy self with energies directly from the sun, aim to consume as many yellow and orange-colored foods as possible, including yellow and orange peppers, mangoes, nectarines, lemons, yellow zucchini, butternut squash, papayas, and oranges. These vibrant hues in living foods offer the same nourishment and replenishment for your aura as a daily dose of cheerful sunshine.

Embrace your butterfly-drinking-nectar-all-day-long-style of eating! Nibble on organic fruits, vegetables, flowers, fruit juices, herbs, berries and dark chocolate. This fairy chapter features delicious recipes for you to create, so take your lunch outside and relish it with the company of squirrels, rabbits, chipmunks, and bird friends who come by to say hello.

carrot sweet potato soup

1 teaspoon avocado oil
1 yellow onion, chopped into chunks
1 teaspoon cinnamon
1 teaspoon turmeric
1 teaspoon paprika
salt and pepper
3 medium carrots, chopped into chunks
4 cups sweet potatoes, peeled and cubed
6 cups chicken broth
Garnishes of chopped green onions, basil, edible flowers, dried cranberries, pumpkin seeds, heavy cream or coconut cream

In a large pot, heat the oil over medium heat, then add in the onions, stirring frequently until they are soft and translucent, about 10 minutes. Add in the spices of cinnamon, turmeric, paprika, salt and pepper. After mixing well, add the carrots, sweet potatoes, and chicken broth.

Bring to a boil, then cover and simmer over medium-low heat until the vegetables are soft, about 25 minutes. Once the vegetables are soft, puree them together using a hand blender until the soup is creamy and smooth. Taste and add more salt and pepper until flavorful.

Serve the soup in a bowl and drizzle with pretty little swirls of heavy cream or coconut cream. Add sprinkles of garnishings and serve with a baguette and butter.

pixie fudge with edible flowers

3 cups (18 oz) dark chocolate chips
1 can sweetened condensed milk (14 oz)
2 tablespoons butter
3 teaspoons instant espresso powder
2 teaspoons cinnamon

Line an 8" square pan with wax paper and butter the wax paper. In a medium saucepan combine all of the ingredients and cook on low, stirring constantly until the mixture is smooth. Remove from the heat and spread evenly in the prepared pan.

Cover and refrigerate for 3 hours until the fudge is set. Remove from the pan and slice into 1" squares. Store at room temperature.

When serving, sprinkle the fudge with edible flowers on a platter such as nasturtium, coneflower, calendula, pansy, or garden phlox, and add dried mandarin orange slices or fresh raspberries around the platter.

fairyberry chicken salad

3 cups of cooked or rotisserie chicken, cut into cubes
1 handful of fresh basil, chopped
1 small handful of garden chives or green onions, chopped
3 cups of fresh fruit including halved red grapes, halved cherries, fresh blueberries, raspberries and blackberries

<u>fairy spice dressing</u>
1 cup mayonnaise
2 tablespoons white vinegar
1/3 cup dark brown sugar
3 tablespoons milk
1 teaspoon paprika
sprinkling of chili powder
1-2 teaspoons garam masala
1 teaspoon dill
1 teaspoon tarragon
1 teaspoon salt, to taste
1 teaspoon pepper, to taste

Add all of the fairy spice dressing ingredients together in a medium size bowl. Thoroughly mix and set aside, allowing the flavors to blend.

In a large bowl, mix together the cubed chicken with the chopped basil, garden chives and green onions. Then drizzle the fairy spice dressing over the top. Mix until well combined. Season to perfection with more salt and pepper.

Gently fold in the fruit until just evenly distributed. Serve on pretty plates garnished with a basil leaf or edible flowers, or between buttery, flaky croissants.

dining

fairies prefer

appetizers, veggies and dips

edible flowers, honey, and chocolate

sipping fruit juices

nature music

snacking all day long

dining in a garden near birds, butterflies,
creeks and waterfalls

lunching near a sunny window

fairy market

carrots
honey
blackberries
zinnias
pumpkin
sunflower oil
dried fruit
dark chocolate
orange calendula petals
nasturtiums
raspberries
tarragon
apricots
purple coneflower petals
orange bell peppers
chives
bee balm flowers
tangerines
pansies
blue violets
yams

dragon aura

Welcome to your dragon aura!

Dragons exude beautiful, loving energy, and here's what you need to know:

You possess one of the most heart-centered spirits. Your mission on Earth is to spread kindness and love, ensuring that justice and goodness prevail. You lovingly protect your family and home, and you may even have dreams about flying. Your spirit might be actively engaged in missions while you sleep, requiring more rest and deeper sleep than others. Sleep, rest, and nourishment are vital to prevent burnout.

To rejuvenate and sustain your innate burning flame, you must nourish yourself with warm, invigorating foods brimming with nutrients, vitamins, fiery hues of living energy, and aromatic spices.

So, fill your dragon-self up with braised, hearty meats and eggs, flavorful stews, warm curries, and vegetables infused with aromatic root spices like ginger, turmeric, garlic, leeks, shallots, and cardamom. These foods will fortify you, granting you the strength to nurture your loved ones before a restful slumber. Enjoy the dragon recipes provided here, as they are created with the energy of love!

coconut red pepper chicken

3 tablespoons ghee or butter
2 pounds chicken breasts, cubed into bite-sized pieces
salt and pepper
1 red bell pepper, diced into bite-sized chunks
½ cup onion, chopped
2 tablespoons tikka curry paste
2 tablespoons garam masala
1 can fire roasted tomatoes
2 tablespoons chicken bouillon base
1 can of coconut milk
garnishes of cilantro and green onions

Heat the ghee on medium heat in a large skillet or Dutch oven on the stove. Add in the chicken with the salt and pepper and cook the chicken for about 5 minutes until it is no longer pink.

Add in the red bell pepper, onions, curry paste, and garam masala and stir, cooking for 2 more minutes. Then add in the can of roasted tomatoes, chicken bouillon base, and a can of coconut milk. Stir everything together and bring to a boil. Turn the heat down to simmer and cover with a lid, simmering for another 15 minutes.

Taste and season to perfection. Serve over jasmine rice or coconut rice and garnish with chopped cilantro and green onions.

black bean avocado bowls

1 cup brown basmati rice
2 large sweet potatoes, 4 cups cubed
¼ cup avocado oil
1 teaspoon paprika
½ teaspoon chili powder
2 red bell peppers
1 can black beans, (preferably cuban style) drained
toppings of chopped cilantro, fresh lime wedges, sliced avocado, sliced jalapeño

spicy dragon dressing:
½ cup greek yogurt
3 tablespoons freshly squeezed lime juice and zest
⅛ teaspoon cumin
¼ teaspoon paprika
½ teaspoon chili powder
1 teaspoon hot sauce
salt and pepper

Preheat the oven to 425 degrees. Cook the rice according to package directions and then let cool. Peel the sweet potatoes, chop them into bite-sized chunks and place in a bowl. Toss with 3 tablespoons of avocado oil, paprika, and chili powder.

Roast the sweet potatoes in the oven on a sheet pan for about 35 minutes or more until tender. Slice the red bell peppers into bite-sized chunks, toss with 1 teaspoon avocado oil, and then roast alongside the sweet potatoes in a small pan for 10 minutes. After removing the sweet potatoes and bell peppers from the oven, allow them both to cool to room temperature. Warm up the drained black beans in a small pot on the stove.

To make the spicy dragon dressing, use a small bowl to combine all of the dressing ingredients (greek yogurt, lime juice and zest, cumin, paprika, chili powder, and hot sauce, salt and pepper) and whisk until thoroughly combined. To make the bowls, fill with the cooled rice, top with colorful sections of the vegetables and black beans, and then add the toppings and drizzle with the spicy dressing.

dragon healing soup

2 tablespoons avocado oil
2 leeks, cleaned and cut into thin slices
3 carrots, cut into small chunks
3 celery stalks, cut into small chunks
2 garlic cloves, chopped
2 tablespoons ginger, grated
½ bunch cilantro, chopped, plus leaves for garnish
6 cups chicken stock (homemade is best)
2 tablespoons soy sauce
2 tablespoons mirin
2 teaspoons salt
2 teaspoons pepper
1 lime, zest and juice
1 teaspoon red pepper flakes
2 pounds of chicken breasts
2-3 heads baby bok choy, cut off ends, and then quarter
small bunch of radishes, each cut into eighths
6 ounces of rice noodles or any asian style noodles
garnishes of sriracha or chili paste, chopped cilantro, purple basil, sweet basil and mint leaves

Heat 2 tablespoons of oil in a large soup pot. Add the leeks, carrots, and celery, and cook until soft. Add in the garlic, ginger, and cilantro, and cook for another 2 minutes. Pour in the chicken stock, soy sauce, mirin, salt, pepper, and ½ of the lime zest and lime juice and red pepper flakes. Add in the whole chicken breasts, bring to a boil, cover, and turn the heat to low and cook for 30 minutes.

Once the chicken breasts have cooked, remove them while the soup is still simmering and allow them to cool on a plate so they can be shredded with two forks once they cool down. Then return the shredded chicken to the soup. Add the other half of the lime zest and lime juice, bok choy, and radishes, and cook for another 10 minutes. Add more seasonings to taste.

When the soup is ready to be served, cook the noodles according to package directions, drain, and place the noodles in soup bowls. Immediately ladle the soup into each bowl and garnish with chili paste and fresh herbs.

dining

dragons prefer

steaming, hot food

many together in a calm, voiceless environment

large, heavy golden or silver cutlery

togetherness of mothers nourishing their children

heavy rectangular picnic tables and benches, wooden tables and chairs

golden, warm light of candles

pottery dinnerware

dragon market

red chiles
black beans
brown basmati rice
soy sauce
coconut milk
leeks
eggs
roasted red bell peppers
mushrooms
avocado
chicken
mint
cloves
cumin
fire roasted tomatoes
paprika
ginger
purple basil
coffee
black pepper
red carrot
garlic

color energies

green color energies

> compassion
> empathy
> contentment
> harmony
> connection to earth

spinach, kiwi, avocado, asparagus, green beans, lime, collard greens, green pear, broccoli, swiss chard, green grapes, green bell pepper, broccolini, romaine lettuce, honeydew melon, green apple

purple and blue color energies

expression
truthfulness
balance
endurance
peace of mind

blue carrots, purple cabbage, figs,
purple grapes, eggplant, dates,
purple potatoes, blueberries, blackberries,
butterfly pea flower tea, and
flowers of borage, bachelor button,
pansy, lavender, voilet and viola

white color energies

hope
calm
grace
openness
inspiration
clarity

cauliflower, garlic, ginger,
jicama, mushrooms, onions,
parsnips, potatoes, turnips,
coconut, flowers of thyme,
mint and cilantro

yellow color energies

joy
health
new beginnings
mental agility

bananas, pears, honey,
egg yolk, lemon, mango, turmeric,
star fruit, yellow wax beans, pineapple,
yellow tomato, acorn squash,
nasturtium flowers,
squash blossoms

orange color energies

creativity
enthusiasm
warm hearted-ness
taking action

apricots, yams, cantaloupe, mango, orange bell pepper, tangerine, sweet potato, papaya, carrots, pumpkin, blossoms of calendula, nasturtium and marigold

red color energies

strength
grounding
courage
energy
warmth

cranberries, red bell pepper, strawberries, raspberries, tomatoes, cherries, beef, hibiscus tea, kidney beans, radishes, beets, red grapes, red geranium, red garden rose

tastes of living colors

acorn squash 88, 95, 132, 133
agave 76
almond milk 90
apricot 135
asian pear 95
asparagus 67, 127
avocado 123, 126, 127
avocado oil 53, 88, 100, 116, 118
bachelor button 129
bacon 16, 25, 58, 67
banana 44, 48, 53, 95, 132, 133
basil 62, 67, 100, 104
bee balm flower 109
beef 72, 137

beef with cauliflower 72

beet 16, 25, 137
black bean 123

black bean avocado bowls 116

blackberry 76, 104, 109, 129
black pepper 90, 104, 118, 123
blue carrot 53, 129
blue potato 53, 128
blue violet 109
blueberry 44, 46, 48, 53, 104, 128, 129

blueberry banana smoothie 48

bok choy 53, 118
borage flower 129
broccoli 25, 127
broccolini 16, 67, 127

brown basmati rice 114, 123
brussels sprouts 25
butter 18, 25, 58, 62, 67, 86, 88, 102
butterfly pea flower tea 129
calendula flower 102, 109, 134, 135
cantaloupe 135
cardamom 90
carrot 100, 109, 118, 134, 135

carrot sweet potato soup 100

cauliflower 72, 81, 130, 131
celery 118
cheddar cheese 86
cherry 76, 81, 104, 136, 137
cherry tomato 32
chicken 62, 104, 114, 118, 123
chicken broth 100, 118
chickpea 30, 39
chili paste 118
chili powder 104, 116
chive 16, 104, 109
cilantro 58, 67, 114, 118
cilantro flower 131
cinnamon 18, 25, 46, 48, 88, 90, 100, 102

cinnamon maple squash 88

clementine 134
clove 90, 123
coconut 18, 53, 131
coconut cream 100
coconut flour 44, 53

coconut flour blueberry pancakes 44

coconut milk 72, 90, 114, 123

coconut red pepper chicken 114

coconut water 48
coffee 123
collard green 25, 127
concord grape 53
coneflower 102
cranberry 81, 100, 137
cream 18, 25, 100
cream cheese 20

crimson red fruit salad 76

cucumber 32, 67
cumin 123
dark chocolate 102, 104, 109
date 39, 129
dill 58, 67, 104

dragon healing soup 118

dried fruit 104
edible flowers 16, 100
egg 18, 44, 86, 95, 123, 133
eggplant 53, 129

elf basil pesto 62

espresso powder 102

fairyberry chicken salad 104

fennel bulb 53
feta cheese 32, 39
fig 34, 39, 129
fire roasted tomato 114, 123

fish 39, 53
fish sauce 53
five spice powder 72
garam masala 104, 114
garden phlox 102
garlic 30, 58, 62, 74, 118, 123, 130, 131
ghee 44, 72, 74, 90, 95, 114
ginger 90, 95, 118, 123, 131
golden apple 95
golden beet 95

golden healing milk 90

grape tomato 58
greek yogurt 39
green apple 67, 127
green bean 58, 67, 126, 127

green beans with bacon 58

green bell pepper 67, 127
green grape 67, 127
green onion 67, 86, 100, 104, 114
green pea 67
green pear 67, 127
herbal tea 39
hibiscus tea 137
honey 76, 90, 95, 109, 133
honeydew melon 126, 127
hot sauce 116
italian seasoning 58
jalapeno pepper 58
jasmine rice 72
jicama 131
kalamata olive 32
kidney bean 137
kiwi 67, 126, 127

lavender flower 129
leek 118, 123, 130
legume 81
lemon 30, 32, 34, 39, 95, 132, 133
lentil 39
lime 58, 67, 76, 118, 127
lime zest 76, 118
mandarin orange 102
mango 39, 133, 134, 135
maple syrup 25, 88
marigold blossom 132, 135

mediterranean platter 32

milk 104
mint 72, 76, 118, 123
mint flower 131
mixed greens 32, 39
mozzarella cheese 20
mushroom 123, 131
mustard 53
nasturtium flower 102, 132, 133, 135
nectarine 95
noodle 20, 25, 62
nutmeg 46, 48, 90
oatmeal 18, 25

oatmeal love cake 18

oat milk 90
okra 39
olive 39
olive oil 30, 32, 39, 62
onion 58, 74, 114, 131
orange bell pepper 109, 134, 135
orange 46, 134

pansy flower 102, 109, 129
papaya 95, 135
paprika 86, 100, 104, 114, 123
parmesan cheese 20, 58, 62
parsley 32, 39, 126
parsnip 25, 130, 131
pear 130, 133

pico de gallo 60

pineapple 95, 133
pita bread 32, 39

pixie fudge with edible flowers 102

plum 53, 128
pomegranate 81
potato 25, 81, 130, 131
pumpkin 95, 104, 135
pumpkin seed 100
purple basil 118, 123
purple cabbage 53, 129
purple carrot 128
purple cauliflower 53
purple grape 53, 128, 129
purple potato 129
quinoa 81
radish 25, 81, 118, 137
rainbow chard 81
raspberry 76, 81, 102, 104, 137
red apple 81
red beet 16
red bell pepper 114, 116, 136, 137
red carrot 123
red chile 123

red curry paste 72
red garden rose 137
red geranium flower 136, 137
red grape 104, 137
red onion 25
red pepper flake 118
rice noodle 118
ricotta cheese 20
roasted red pepper 30, 32, 39, 123

roasted red pepper hummus 30

romaine lettuce 127
rosemary 74, 81
sage 25
salmon 46

salmon with blueberry sauce 46

sausage 20
shallot 25
sheep's milk cheese 39
smoked gouda cheese 16
spaghetti sauce 20
spinach 20, 25, 67, 81, 86, 126, 127

spinach cream cheese lasagna 20

squash blossom 133
sriracha sauce 118
star fruit 95, 133
strawberry 76, 81, 136, 137
summer squash 95
sunflower oil 104
sunflower seed 16, 25

sunshine tortilla eggs 86

sweet basil 118
sweet potato 16, 25, 100, 114, 134, 135

sweet potato bird nest bowls 16

swiss chard 127
tahini paste 30, 39
tangerine 109, 135
tarragon 104
tortilla 86
thyme 53
thyme flower 131
tikka curry paste 114
tomato 39, 81, 136, 137
turkey 53, 81
turmeric 90, 95, 100, 133
turnip 25, 131
vanilla 18, 25, 34, 48, 90
vanilla bean pod 48, 53

vanilla fig jam 34

viola flower 129
violet flower 129
watermelon 76, 81, 136
white hard cheese 67
white onion 58, 67, 81
yam 109, 135
yellow bell pepper 86, 95, 132
yellow onion 100
yellow tomato 95, 133
yellow wax bean 133
yellow zucchini 95
yogurt 48

yukon gold medallions 74

yukon gold potato 74
zinnia flower 109
zucchini blossom 132
zucchini noodle 53

edible flowers

honorable mentions

bachelor button
bee balm
borage
butterfly pea flower
calendula
cilantro flower
coneflower
garden phlox
garden rose
geranium
hibiscus
lavender
marigold
mint flower
nasturtium
thyme flower
pansy
viola
violet
zinnia
zucchini squash blossom

 kerrylewiscolor.com

@kerry_lewis_color_

Want to tap into your intuitive essence through food? Let Kerry guide you toward a flavorful adventure that nourishes your soul and revitalizes every facet of your life.

www.ingramcontent.com/pod-product-compliance
Lightning Source LLC
Chambersburg PA
CBHW041417010526
44107CB00016B/1204